Edvard Grieg
(1843-1907)

Lyriske stykker
Lyric Pieces · Lyrische Stücke · Pièces lyriques

II

for piano · für Klavier · pour piano

Revised edition

Urtext

Edited by · Herausgegeben von · Edité par
Thomas Aßmus & Tamás Zászkaliczky
K 106 B
Könemann Music Budapest

INDEX
I

Svunne dager

Vanished Days – Entschwundene Tage – Jours écoulés

Op. 57, No. 1.

K 106 B

Da Capo al Fine

Gade

K 106 B

Illusion

Allegretto serioso

Hemmelighet
Secret – Geheimnis – Mystère

Op. 57, No. 4.

K 106 B

Hun danser

She Dances – Sie tanzt – Elle danse

Op. 57, No. 5.

K 106 B

Hjemve
Home-sickness – Heimweh – Mal du pays

Op. 57, No. 6.

(tre corde)

poco a poco più lento al Fine

rit.

28

Sylfide

Op. 62, No. 1.

Takk
Gratitude – Dank – Gratitude

Op. 62, No. 2.

K 106 B

K 106 B

Fransk serenade

French Serenade – Französische Serenade – Sérénade française

Op. 62, No. 3.

K 106 B

Bekken
Brooklet – Bächlein – Ruisseau

Op. 62, No. 4.

38

K 106 B

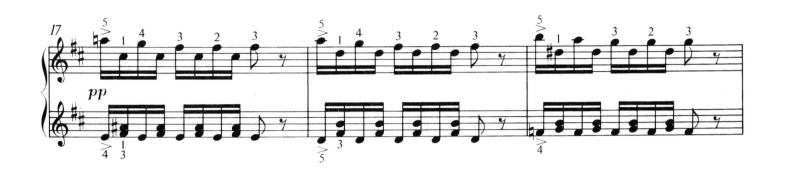

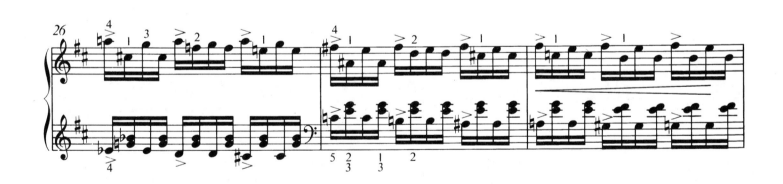

K 106 B

Drømmesyn

Phantom – Traumgesicht – Vision

Poco andante ed espressivo

Op. 62, No. 5.

K 106 B

Hjemad
Homeward – Heimwärts – Vers la patrie

Op. 62, No. 6.

Fra ungdomsdagene

From Early Years – Aus jungen Tagen – De la jeunesse

Allegro moderato e tranquillo

Op. 65, No. 1.

Bondens sang

Peasant's Song – Lied des Bauern – Chant du paysan

Op. 65, No. 2.

Tungsinn
Melancholy – Schwermut – Mélancolie

Op. 65, No. 3.

50.

K 106 B

Salon

Allegretto con grazia

51.

I balladetone

Ballad – Im Balladenton – Ballade

Lento lugubre

Op. 65, No. 5.

K 106 B

Bryllupsdag på Troldhaugen

Wedding-day at Troldhaugen – Hochzeitstag auf Troldhaugen –
Jour de noces au Troldhaugen

Op. 65, No. 6.

Tempo di Marcia (un poco vivace)

K 106 B

Matrosenes oppsang

Sailors' Song – Matrosenlied – Chant des matelots

Allegro vivace e marcato

Op. 68, No. 1.

54.

K 106 B

Bestemors menuett

Grandmother's Minuet – Großmutters Menuett – Menuet de la grand'mère

Allegretto grazioso e leggierissimo

Op. 68, No. 2.

K 106 B

For dine føtter

At your Feet – Zu deinen Füßen – A tes pieds

Poco andante e molto espressivo

Op. 68, No. 3.

K 106 B

Aften på høyfjellet

Evening in the Mountains – Abend im Hochgebirge – Soir dans les montagnes

Op. 68, No. 4.

82

Bådnlåt

At the Cradle – An der Wiege – Au berceau

Op. 68, No. 5.

K 106 B

Valse mélancolique

Op. 68, No. 6.

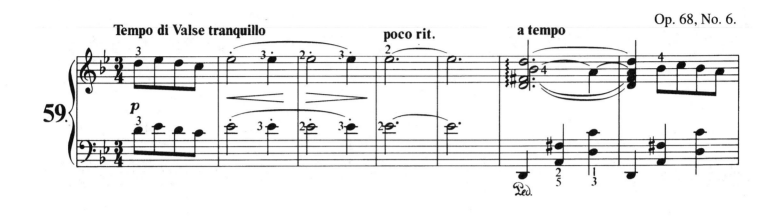

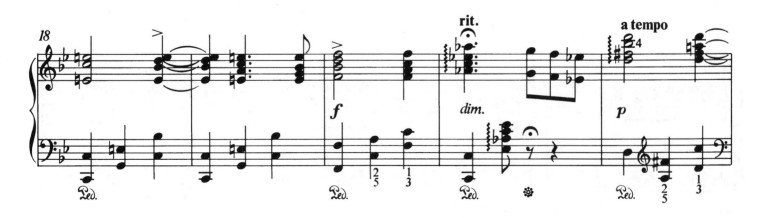

K 106 B

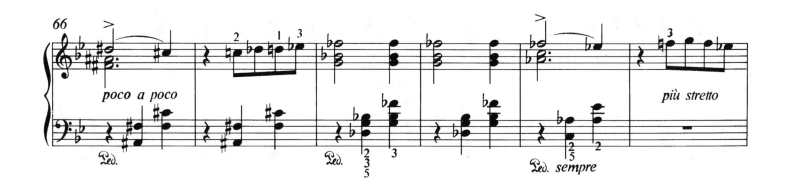

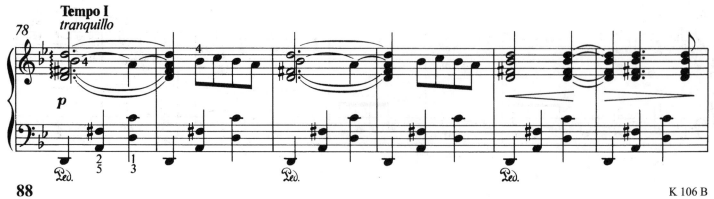

K 106 B

Det var engang

Once upon a Time – Es war einmal – Il y avait une fois

Andante con moto, ♩=63
Im schwedischen Volkston

Op. 71, No. 1.

Sommeraften

Summer's Eve – Sommerabend – Soir d'été

Allegretto tranquillamente, ♩ = 69

Op. 71, No. 2.

61.

Småtroll

Puck – Kobold – Lutin

Op. 71, No. 3.

100

Skogstillhet

Peace of the Woods – Waldesstille – Repos de forêt

Op. 71, No. 4.

Halling

Norwegian Dance – Norwegischer Tanz – Danse norwégienne

K 106 B

Forbi

Gone – Vorüber – Passé

Op. 71, No. 6.

Efterklang

Remembrances – Nachklänge – Souvenirs

Op. 71, No. 7.

K 106 B